DENIS WRIGLEY

The living world of the
RIVER

A Wrigley Eye Opener

LUTTERWORTH PRESS
Guildford and London

2

Look at the gleam and glisten
of the river.
Water on the move — splashing
and gurgling its way
to the sea.

Have you ever looked at a river
and the life that lives in it
and round it
and because of it?

Have you?

A river starts where water collects.
Water that comes from rain or melted snows
soaks into the ground
and settles in hollows.
The ground becomes so full of water
that the hollows, little hollows, big hollows
middle sized hollows, fill up,
making puddles or pools or lakes.
But sooner or later there just isn't room
for the water...
and out it pours...

Water finds its own level,
flowing downwards.
From the first trickle
to the rivulet
that grows into a stream
and then, downwards still,
this flow becomes a river
as it moves towards the sea.

The river
is a lot of different things —
a home for living things
and a place of food
and drink, and a means of
draining the land.

6

It changes its character
as it travels down to the sea,
and as it changes
it provides different conditions
for the lives of fish, plants, insects
and animals that live in it
and around it.

As it travels down to the sea
a river flows at different speeds.
The speed of the river is called
its current.
Steep slopes cause fast currents
and so do narrow channels.
The faster the force of water,
the more quickly
it wears away the rocks
to make a channel.

8

Soft rocks wear away quickly,
hard rocks slowly.
The force of the water
affects everything it moves against —
making pebbles smooth
and round as they are rubbed
against each other,
and catching anything loose
and carrying it in the
current.

The power of water
to wear away the land
is great.
This is how deep valleys
have been made
over many years

A river rushes and tumbles
from the hills,
down steep and rocky places
and through narrow channels.
It races over rocks,
over boulders...
moving fast.

Nothing much can grow here —
only mosses can cling to the rocks.
Larvae — that's the name for
the creatures, just emerged
from the egg,
that one day will turn into insects —
can live here
among the frothing, bubbling
beginnings of the river.

12

So there's not much life
in the early stages
of the river,
but when the river widens a little
fish can live in the waters
and eat the larvae.
Here they also come
to lay their eggs.

Fish make different kinds of nests and protect their eggs
in different ways. Here the male makes a shallow nest
in the mud; the female lays the eggs; then the male stays
on guard till they hatch.

Another way to protect the eggs
is to hide them under stones;
fish that do this then leave them to hatch alone.

As the ground becomes less steep
and the river reaches
the broad, green valley
it flows more slowly,
more gently.
In deep pools
and quiet inlets
fish and other life
lie hidden.

Here the twigs and stones
that have been carried along
by the fast-moving water
drop to the muddy bottom
of the river
or become stuck on the mud
and pebbles
where the slow moving water gets
shallow.

The water here isn't so cold
as it was in the high land
but there's plenty of oxygen
for the animal life in it.
There's more plant life, too,
providing more food for fish.

Water birds can build their nests
here and seeds,
blown by the breeze,
can come to rest to grow into clumps
of green on the muddy banks.
In the quiet waters, where the stones
make shadows,
fish lie hidden.

Some birds build their nests
of twigs in the reeds
on the muddy silt
left by the slowing river water.
Other birds make their nests
in holes in the bank
or in the tall reeds.
There are nests, too, hidden
in the leafy branches nearby.
Hidden and protected from
their enemies each bird
builds a nest suited
to its life in or on or by the river.

So with more food,
warmer water and water
that's not moving so swiftly,
there are good conditions
for more kinds of fish.
And also for the birds and animals
which catch them...!

Look!
There, where the water
was so still a moment ago!
Look at those bubbles
and the rings of ripples.

Can you guess what it was?

It was a fish that had been hiding
deep in the stones or mud
of the river bottom...
waiting...waiting...

waiting and watching...
for a fly to settle
on the water's surface.
In one swift movement
fish and fly have disappeared!
The ripples are gone
and the water is still
and mirror like,
reflecting the overhanging
branches of the
river bank

Insects are plentiful by the river
and provide food for the birds and fishes.
Most insects have four stages to their life.
The egg, the larva, when no wings
can be seen, the pupa, when it is resting,
and then the winged insect.
Some have four wings,
beetles two, for the other
two have hardened to
become protective wing cases.
Many insects only have three stages
egg, nymph, adult. Some of these nymphs
live in the water
before developing —
dragonflies for example.

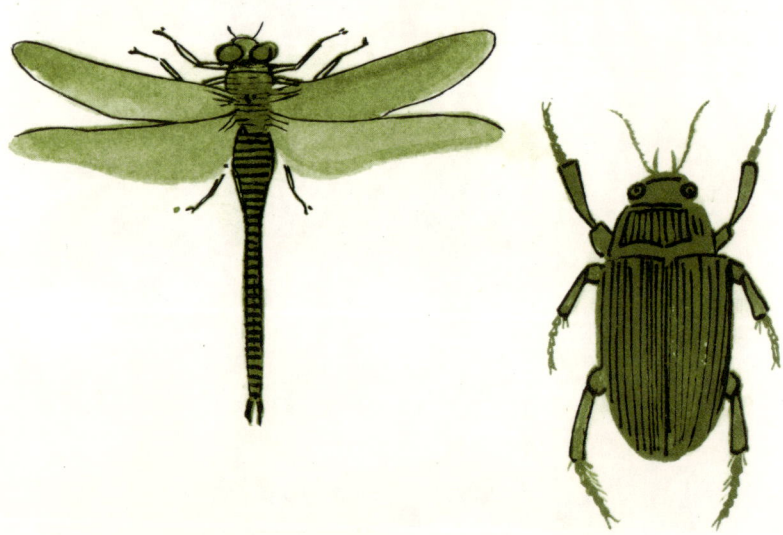

Plants and trees that need the water,
fish and flies
and flowers,
all have their home
where the river is gentle.
Although plants and little fish and insects
lead entirely different lives
they often end up as food for something else!

A fish has no limbs...
it swims by wriggling.
Its fins keep it upright and control
its direction.

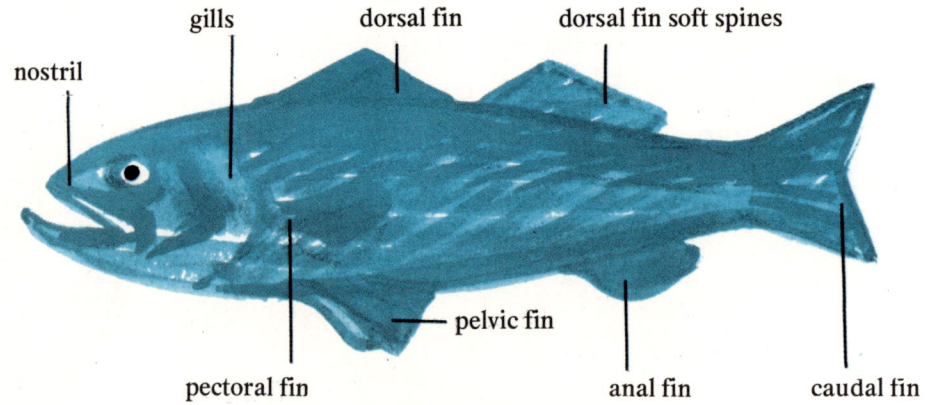

In the green underwater world
of the river
plants grow upwards,
some to break the surface
and flower.
They need oxygen for life.
Those with leaves above the surface
breathe in oxygen from the air
through pores in their leaves.
Plants whose leaves sit on the water
have pores only on the upper side
and those whose leaves
are all under the water
absorb oxygen directly
from the water.

Above the water's surface insects dance
in the sunlight.
In a flash of colour birds swoop
in flight to catch them.
The birds of the river are fish catchers
too!
Look how their beaks are shaped,
each for the work it has to do —
pointed to spear, shovel shaped
to dig in the mud
or shaped to catch insects
or pierce nuts.
Birds also have feet of different shapes,
for swimming, splaying out on mud
or grasping branches.

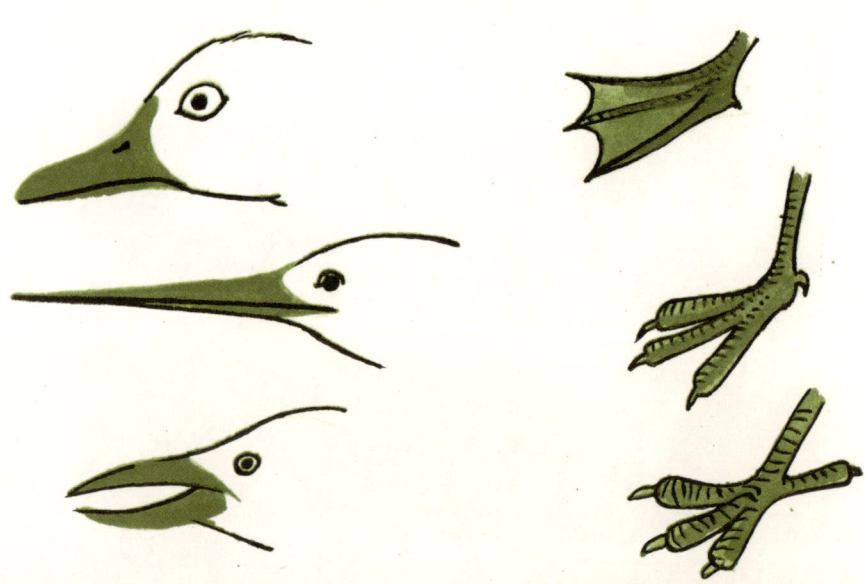

So this is the life of the river,
a balance of life that depends
on the existence of each part.
From the tree roots that bind
the earth of the banks
and provide hiding places
for small animals,
for fishes under the water
and for insects in their bark,
to the flowers and grasses and reeds
edging the water where
butterflies insects, frogs
and snakes may be found.

The river is a source of drinking water
for the life living by it.
Animals come down to drink
leaving their footprints in the mud
for you to see.

There are animals of the river,
often happier in the water
than out of it!
Superb swimmers, they sometimes
swim under water leaving only
a trail of bubbles to
let you know they are there.
The animals of the river are shy
but you see them if you stay still
and watch
and listen.

The water vole
and the otter
are examples of animals
that live in
and by the river

River life changes
as the seasons pass by.
Sunshine and rain,
heat and cold all affect the river
and also the life that exists there.
The rains on the high ground
bring more waters to swell
the river, till sometimes
it bursts out beyond its banks.
Animals and birds fly from their homes
that lie drowned beneath the flood.

Flat land that often is flooded
is called marshland.
Here in the damp conditions
water-loving plants grow
and the area is full of many
reptiles and insects and the birds
that feed upon them.

When the river lies under rainless
skies and the hot sun,
it can dry up and become
a mere trickle.
Plants and animal life suffer
from lack of water and the mud and silt
harden to form barriers when the flow starts
again.
These barriers are the cause
of the changing course
of the river.
The curving river is changed
as the water cuts into the outer curve
and the silt falls in the inner curve.

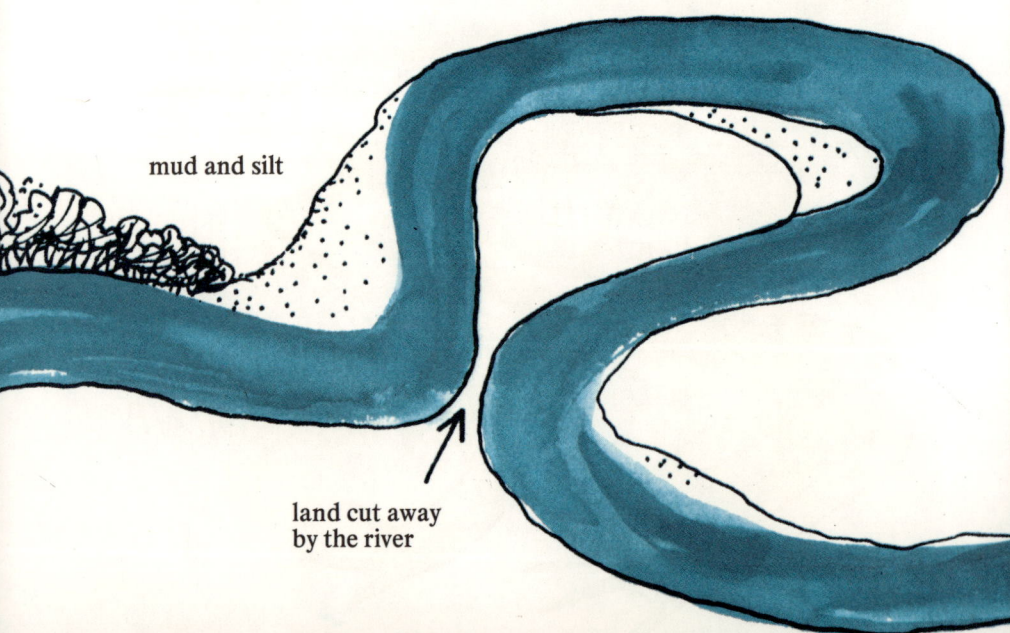

Watch for these signs
of the changing seasons and
the changing life of the river.
Look and listen for the sights and
sounds of new life, young birds
and animals.
See if you can find out
more of the secrets of
this world of the river.
Have you, for instance ever seen
an insect walking
on the water?
Have you?

And how did it do it?

First published 1977
Copyright © 1977 Denis Wrigley
ISBN 0 7188 2202 1
Printed in Hong Kong